mᵛ

A New True Book

THE PENOBSCOT

By Jill Duvall

CHILDRENS PRESS®

CHICAGO

Penobscot ceremonial apron

Project Editor: Fran Dyra
Design: Margrit Fiddle

PHOTO CREDITS
American Philosophical Society Library, Frank G.
Speck Collection—7 (left), 8, 9 (top left), 10 (right),
11 (top left), 13 (2 photos), 14, 15 (left), 16 (left),
17 (left), 18 (right), 33

The Bettmann Archive—7 (right)

© Reinhard Brucker—25 (right); Field Museum,
Chicago, 9 (bottom left and right), 17 (right)

© Jerry Hennen—Cover

© Emilie Lepthien—10 (left)

National Baseball Library & Archive, Cooperstown,
N.Y.—36 (left)

North Wind Picture Archives—11 (top right), 20,
21, 23 (2 photos)

North Wind Pictures—12 (top left), 18 (left), 26;
Maine State Museum, 16 (right)

Root Resources—© Mark Sisco, Penobscot Indian
Nation Museum, Cover Inset; © Mark Sisco, 34
(2 photos); © Mark Sisco, Hudson Museum,
University of Maine, Orono, 2, 9 (top right), 11
(bottom left), 45 (left); © Alan G. Nelson, 12 (right);
© The Pierce Studio, Richard Bancroft, 45 (right)

SuperStock International, Inc.—© A. Rakoczy, 4

UPI/Bettmann—6 (2 photos), 15 (right), 25 (left),
29, 31, 32, 36 (right), 39 (2 photos), 40, 43
(2 photos)

Valan—© J. A. Wilkinson, 12 (bottom left)

Horizon Graphics—Map, 4

Cover: 70-year-old Old Town canoe made of wood
and canvas

Cover Inset: Headdress [Old John Neptune's]

Library of Congress Cataloging-in-Publication Data

Duvall, Jill.
    The Penobscot / by Jill Duvall.
        p.   cm. — (A New true book)
    Includes index.
    Summary: Describes the history, culture, and
changing fortunes of the Penobscot Indians.
    ISBN 0-516-01194-4
    1. Penobscot Indians—Juvenile literature.
[1. Penobscot Indians. 2. Indians of North
America.] I. Title.
E99.P5D88 1993
973'.04973—dc20   93-796
                                       CIP
                                       AC

TABLE OF CONTENTS

MAINE

Penobscot River

Augusta ★

The Penobscot River

PEOPLE OF THE ROCKY RIVER

The Penobscot is the longest river in Maine. It flows 350 miles through the center of the state and empties into the Atlantic Ocean.

The river was named for the Penobscots—Native Americans who lived along its banks for thousands of years. The Penobscots called themselves *Panawampskik*, which

The Penobscot of Maine in 1925

means "People of the
Rocky River."

In 1604, a French
explorer named Samuel de
Champlain came to the
Penobscot territory.
Champlain and his men
saw many Penobscot

6

Samuel de Champlain (inset) visited the Penobscot villages in 1604.

villages as their ship
sailed far up the river.
   The Native Americans
invited the French explorers
to come ashore. Soon
they were making friends
with people who were very
different from themselves.

7

The Penobscots built small wigwams
at their hunting camps.

A YEAR OF PENOBSCOT LIFE

The villages along the river were not the only homes of the Penobscots. They had several camps that they visited at least once during the year.

In the spring, most of the families lived in wigwams along the river. A wigwam was a frame of poles covered with sheets of bark. The Penobscots planted crops and made clothes, canoes, and tools. They also tapped the maple trees for sweet sap,

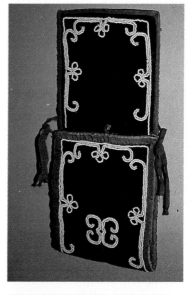

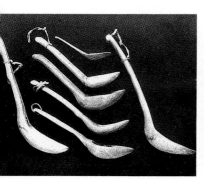

The Penobscots made useful and beautiful everyday things such as spoons and ladles (above left), birchbark trays (above center), collars and cuffs (above right), and beaded pouches (top right).

Corn and squash were important crops for the Penobscots. Woven baskets (above) were used to carry vegetables and fruits.

which they traded with other tribes.

After planting beans, squash, corn, and other vegetables, the Penobscots packed their canoes and paddled down the river to the seashore. Here, the men caught many kinds of fish. Some of the catch was dried and stored in baskets to be saved for winter. The children helped look for clams, crabs, lobsters, and oysters.

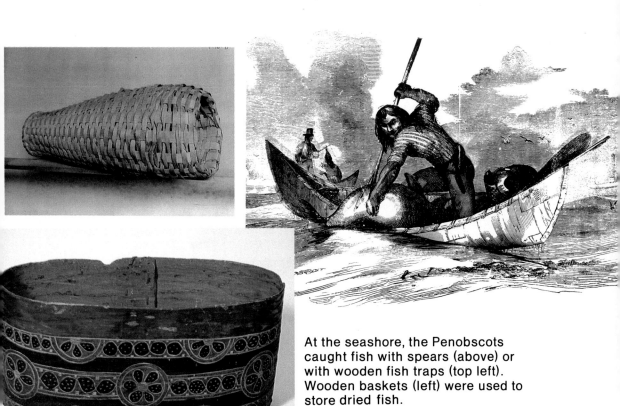

At the seashore, the Penobscots caught fish with spears (above) or with wooden fish traps (top left). Wooden baskets (left) were used to store dried fish.

Many wild fruits such as blueberries (top left) and chokecherries (left) grew in Penobscot territory. Shorebird nests (above) provided fresh eggs.

The Penobscots also gathered fruits. Wild grapes, cherries, berries, and other fruits grew everywhere. Sometimes the women and children collected fresh eggs from shorebird nests.

Birchbark canoes were light and sturdy boats for traveling on rivers and streams. They were built by covering a frame of wood with sheets of birchbark (inset).

When summer was almost over, the families loaded their canoes and paddled back up the river. It was time to harvest the crops they had planted.

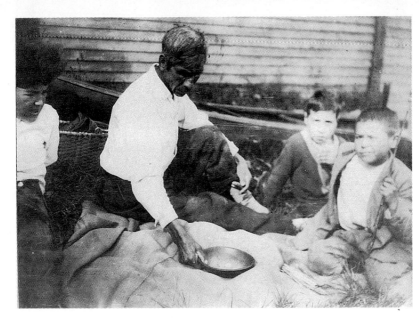

Men and boys playing a bowl and dice game

After the harvest, the Penobscots enjoyed music and dancing. Drums and flutes accompanied the dancers. Dried gourds with pumpkin seeds inside made perfect rattles. They also played games, such as lacrosse.

At night, around the

Young Penobscots learned
about the history and
beliefs of their tribe
from stories told
by the old people.

autumn fires, the old
people told many
wonderful stories about
animals and the sacred
beings of nature. In this
way, Penobscot children
learned about the ideas
and beliefs of their people. **15**

Hunters used birchbark moose calls (left) to hunt moose. They hunted caribou (right) in the northern part of their territory.

In the fall, the people went hunting and trapping. They traveled to the forests farther north. Moose, deer, caribou, bear, and many other animals were plentiful there. Smaller animals around the winter camp included otter, muskrat, beaver, and rabbit.

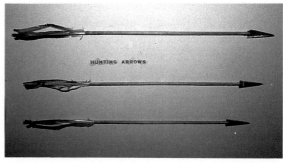

Left: A rack used for
scraping animal skins
Above: Penobscot arrows

Penobscot families
camped in the woods.
They made shelters from
tree branches and used
animal furs to keep out
the cold.

Boys and girls were
taught to make snares, set
traps, and shoot with bows
and arrows.

17

The Penobscots used snowshoes to travel over the ice and snow in winter.

In the winter, ice and
snow covered the land.
The Penobscots traveled
on snowshoes and sleds.
It was time for the families
to return to their villages
along the Penobscot River.

FRIENDS AND ENEMIES

After Champlain's visit, French fur traders came to the Penobscot territory. The fur traders learned from the Indians and adopted their life-style. Like the Native Americans, they wanted only to use the land. They did not want to own it. After each hunting season, most traders went home to Europe and sold their pelts.

The French fur traders welcomed the Native Americans to their camps.

The Penobscots and the French fur traders got along well. But the next group to arrive in Penobscot territory made friendship difficult.

English ships were loaded

The English treated the Native Americans as enemies. Here, dogs are shown chasing people away from the English settlement.

with people planning to stay. They believed they had every right to own land in Penobscot territory.

Soon there was conflict between the settlers and the Native Americans who wanted the same land. During this troubled time, the French sided with the American Indians against the English settlers.

CHANGES FOR THE TRIBE

Roman Catholic priests called Jesuits came to America with the French explorers. They lived among the Penobscots and tried to teach them about Christianity.

The Penobscots soon began blending their own spiritual ideas and ceremonies with those of the Catholic faith. This caused even more conflict

The Jesuit fathers (left) brought the Catholic faith to the Penobscots. The Indians combined Catholic beliefs with their own religious ceremonies (right).

with the English, who were mostly Protestants.

In Europe, Catholics and Protestants had fought about religion for many years. And the fighting did not stop when they moved away from their homelands.

WABANAKI

Many different people lived in the Penobscot territory. Small family bands had formed larger tribes. These tribes often joined in agreements for peace and trade with other groups.

The Penobscots were part of one of these larger groups. They called themselves *Wabanaki*, which means "People of the Dawn." The major

Passamaquoddy Indians take part in a celebration of the three-hundredth anniversary of the English Pilgrims' landing at Plymouth Rock. Inset: a Micmac basket decorated with porcupine quills.

tribes of the Wabanaki were the Micmac, Malecite, Passamaquoddy, and Penobscot.

Each Wabanaki tribe had its own territory on a major river. The land along

A bull moose. Moose were one of the large forest animals hunted by the Penobscots.

the riverbanks and back into the forests was used by the tribe who lived there. If others wanted to use the land for hunting, trapping, or fishing, they had to ask that tribe for permission.

One of the neighboring groups was called the Iroquois Confederacy.

Many stories tell of the
fighting between the
Wabanaki and the Iroquois.
Some of the fights arose
because the Native
Americans were supporting
different groups of Europeans.

But something much
worse came with the
Europeans. They brought
diseases. The Native
Americans had no
resistance against these
diseases. As a result,
thousands of people died.
Many tribes were wiped out.

LOSING THEIR FRENCH FRIENDS

Between 1689 and 1763, the French and English fought four wars over their land claims in the North American colonies. These were called the French and Indian Wars. The English finally defeated the French, and the French agreed to leave Canada and the English Colonies.

After the United States became an independent

Louis Solar,
a Penobscot

nation, the Penobscot territory became part of the state of Massachusetts. The new U.S. government promised the Native Americans that no more of their land would be taken. A number of treaties were drawn up and signed.

At first, the U.S. government respected the treaties. The tribes were treated very much as the state governments were treated. But in the last half of the 1800s, many promises were broken. Throughout the United States, non-Indian settlers were given at least two-thirds of the Indian lands.

Soon there were only about 300 Penobscots still

A Penobscot family at Maine's centennial celebration in 1920

in their old territory. They
were left with fewer than
5,000 acres of land for
hunting, fishing, and
farming. The land that was
left was all on islands in
the Penobscot River.

31

Penobscot children at school on Indian Island in 1921

No longer could seasonal
migration be made. Their
way of life was gone and
they had to live as the new
settlers wanted them to.
It seemed to be the end
of Penobscot society.

Indian Island

A NATION WITH HEROES

Their lives changed
dramatically, but the
Penobscots did not
disappear. Indian Island in
the Penobscot River is still
the center of life for the
Penobscots. Today, many

Jerry Pardilla, tribal governor of the Penobscot Nation in 1993, and the tribal courtroom on Indian Island

Penobscots work in pulp, paper, and lumber mills and in shoe factories.

In the past, tribal chiefs inherited their position from fathers or male relatives. Today, the tribal council is elected. It is headed by a governor and a lieutenant governor.

34

The governor of the Penobscot Nation serves for two years. It is not an easy job. The tribe's territory is within the boundaries of the state of Maine. The state and the U.S. government have passed many laws that govern the lives of Native Americans.

The small graveyard outside Penobscot village on Indian Island is a reminder of their French friends of long ago.

Louis Sockalexis (left) in 1900. The great baseball player could throw a ball 400 feet! His cousin, Andrew Sockalexis, is second from right in the picture on the right.

Many names on the tombstones are Indian versions of French names, such as Sockalexis, Attien, and Socabesin. Sockalexis is the name of two men who brought great pride to their nation. Andrew Sockalexis was chosen by the 1912 U.S. Olympic marathon team to compete in Stockholm, Sweden.

His cousin, Louis Sockalexis, was a famous baseball player. An expert hitter, fielder, and base runner, he played for the Cleveland Spiders, a National League team.

After Louis died, the Cleveland team was renamed the Cleveland Indians in his honor.

VICTORY IN THE COURTS

Today, changes are taking place in the Penobscot Nation. They began with a "sit-in." Passamaquoddy and Penobscot tribes decided to hold on to their last few acres and resist any more takeovers. So they blocked the roads leading into their territory, where non-Indians were cutting brush and

In 1969, Passamaquoddys blocked roads (left) to protest Maine state Indian policies. Sixteen-year-old Regina Nicholas (right) was removed from the road by force.

trees to build more vacation homes.

A young lawyer, Thomas Tureen, helped the Penobscots. He decided to prove in U.S. courts that

39

their land had been taken illegally. His argument was based on an old law—the Nonintercourse Act of 1790. That law said all dealings with Native Americans had to be approved by the U.S. Congress.

Thomas Tureen (left) and Joseph Brennan (right), Maine's attorney general, debate about land ownership.

The state government used two arguments against the Penobscots. First, they said the Nonintercourse Act did not include Indians who lived in the original Thirteen Colonies.

Second, the treaties had been signed by Massachusetts. Maine did not become a separate state until 1820. Before then, it was part of Massachusetts. Therefore, they claimed that the

government of Maine had
not violated the treaties.

But Thomas Tureen did
not give up. And on
January 20, 1975, U.S.
district judge Edward T.
Gignoux agreed with him.
Then, on December 23,
1976, the First Circuit
Court of Appeals agreed
with Judge Gignoux. The
Native Americans' claim
was just.

On October 10, 1980,
President Jimmy Carter
signed a complicated

President Carter (left) signing a bill that settled a land claims dispute between the Penobscot and Passamaquoddy people and the state of Maine. District Judge Edward T. Gignoux (right) upheld the Native Americans' land claims in the First Circuit Court of Appeals.

law. It gave the Passamaquoddy and the Penobscots the right to buy back their land. The government provided eighty-one million dollars for the purchases. No one would be made to give back land.

It was a great victory for the small Penobscot Nation. It will now have a territory of 150,000 acres or more.

New homes, churches, businesses, schools, and clinics are being built. And something even more wonderful is happening. Scholars are busy studying the Penobscot language—in Europe!

From the early records of Jesuit priests, the

A painting of Autumn Leaf, a Penobscot ancestor (left)
Modern Old Town canoes (right), made with canvas and nails
rather than the traditional birchbark, are built by the
Penobscot Nation and sold all over the world.

people of the Penobscot
Nation are learning the
language of their
ancestors. After five
hundred years, it seems
that some of the wounds
are beginning to heal.

WORDS YOU SHOULD KNOW

ancestors (AN • sess • terz) — grandparents, or forebears who lived long ago

boundaries (BOUND • reez) — limits; lines that mark the edges of a certain place

canoe (kuh • NOO) — a small boat made from a hollowed-out log or from a wooden frame covered with sheets of bark

caribou (KAIR • ih • boo) — a large deer that lives in the northern parts of North America

Catholic (KATH • lik) — a member of a Christian church whose head lives in Rome, Italy

ceremonies (SAIR • ih • moh • neez) — celebrations or religious services

confederacy (kun • FED • er • uh • see) — a union of nations, states, or people joined together for some purpose

conflict (KAHN • flikt) — a fight; a disagreement

council (COWN • sil) — a meeting held to discuss problems and to decide a course of action

explorer (ex • PLOR • er) — a person who travels to far-off places to learn about the land and the people there

gourd (GORD) — a vegetable like a squash that has a hard, shell-like skin

illegally (il • LEE • gil • ee) — acting against the law

independent (in • dih • PEN • dint) — not controlled by another person or country

inherit (in • HAIR • it) — to receive an office or something of value from a parent or other ancestor

Iroquois (EAR • ih • kwoi) — a group of Native American nations

Jesuit (JEH • zoo • it) — a Catholic priest who belongs to the Society of Jesus

lacrosse (la • KRAWSS) — a game played by teams who try to get a ball into a goal using long sticks with a net at one end

pelt (PEHLT) — fur; the skin of an animal with the fur attached

Protestant (PRAH • tes • tent) — a member of any of several Christian churches that are not allied with the Catholic church

resist (re • ZIST) — to fight against; to oppose

settlers (SET • lerz) — people who come to a new country and establish farms or other homes there

snowshoe (SNOH • shoo) — a light frame of willow wood with leather strips woven across it

territory (TAIR • ih • tor • ee) — an area with definite boundaries that an animal lives in

treaty (TREE • tee) — a written agreement between two groups, having to do with trade, peace, land rights, etc.

version (VER • zhun) — a particular form of a thing, such as a version of the Bible

violate (VY • uh • lait) — to break a law or an agreement

wigwam (WIG • wawm) — a frame of poles covered with sheets of bark

INDEX

About the Author

Jill Duvall is a political scientist who received an M.A. from Georgetown University in 1976. Since then, her research and writing have included a variety of national and international issues. Among these are world hunger, alternative energy, human rights, cross-cultural and interracial relationships. One of her current endeavors is a study of ancient goddess cultures. Ms. Duvall proudly serves as a member of the Board of Managers of the Glen Mills Schools, a facility that is revolutionizing methods for rehabilitating male juvenile delinquents.